Lay Servants Tell Stories

Advanced Course

Ray Buckley

I0792578

DISCIPLESHIP
RESOURCES
NASHVILLE

Cover Design by Nanci Lamar

Cover Illustration "Shadow Horses" by Carter O. Bock

Cover Beadwork created by unknown Oneida artist, from the collection of JoAnn Catolster Eslinger

Edited by Linda R. Whited and David Whitworth

ISBN: 978-0-88177-408-5

DR408

CONTENTS

A Word of Welcome 4

To the Course Leader 6

To the Course Participant 9

Session 1: The Legacy of Storytelling 10

Session 2: Storytelling as Preaching and Testimony 13

Session 3: The Storyteller 16

Session 4: Storysharing 18

Session 5: Telling Our Stories 21

Additional Helpful Resources 23

A Word of Welcome

Storytelling is an invitation. It is an invitation to experience the world of the storyteller, but also an invitation to enter into the story and make it your own. Storytelling is not just the telling of a story but a welcoming into a place of trust, imagination, and personal encounter. It can be an intimate and emotional experience. The sharing of a story is a welcoming.

Storytelling spans all ages and occupations. It is an art form and a means of proclamation for both laity and clergy. In a pragmatic sense, there is no difference between the ordained storyteller and those "ordained to share stories." You are entering into the oldest and most significant means of sharing culture. You are also entering into one of the most effective means of sharing the Good News.

Storytelling as an art form is experiencing a revival throughout the world. Within storytelling, people are reconnecting to their cultures and the face-to-face intimacy of sharing stories. In an age of mass communication, storytelling, simply put, reconnects us with each other. It has been, and still is, a way to connect people to people, and people to God.

As you will find in these five sessions, the role of the storyteller is to be much more than an entertainer of children. In most cultures, the storyteller holds a position of prominence and esteem. The techniques with which you will become acquainted will be valuable in every aspect of your life. The process of story telling is a remarkable gift. Throughout your lifetime, as a storyteller, you will acquire better observation and listening skills, a stronger ability to share your thoughts in the most effective manner, the ability to see people in terms of relationship, and an understanding of communication from the perspective of your audience. You will also begin to recognize stories in the world around you, finding illustration value in simple things, and develop a sense of personal integrity in regard to what you share through story and how you choose to live.

Why is storytelling an Advanced Course in the Lay Servant Ministries program of The United Methodist Church? In essence, it is because the art of story telling, within the context of the church, requires certain skills. Within a faith community, a storyteller needs to be comfortable with basic public speaking, preaching, biblical study, worship, and the history of the church. All of those elements and disciplines represent the "climate" in which you will serve as a storyteller and the traditions upon which you will draw. In many cultures of the world, a storyteller preserves and challenges culture at the highest level. This is particularly true within the church. As a storyteller in the faith community, you need to be intimately familiar with your culture.

There is also the spiritual element of storytelling. To share one's faith experience through story, or to share stories that will impact the faith of others, requires both commitment and spiritual accountability. Story telling in a faith community is not the beginning of discipleship; it is an expression born out of the discipleship experience. Your use of story will be as effective as your commitment to the values embodied within the story. Some valuable questions to ask yourself before these next few hours begin would be: What have my faith experiences led me to believe? Am I committed enough to those beliefs to be an effective sharer, or storyteller, of those beliefs to others? Am I willing to allow God to use not just my words but also the person I am in order to influence others and encourage them in their faith?

Storytelling in a faith community is also an invitation to know God. We are pray-ers of stories. We are sharers of stories. In the end, we have offered our knowledge and ourselves and opened the door for the story to be continued in the life of another. The ending of the story is not ours. We have experienced the same story into which we invite others with confidence.

As you prepare for this time together, do so prayerfully. Pray for God's guidance as you examine and select stories. Pray for the gift of memory as you search your experiences and those that have been offered by others. Pray for the other members of your class as you go through this time together.

Welcome to a time of learning, laughing, sharing, and telling your story. It will be an exciting adventure!

To the Course Leader

GETTING STARTED

Our goal in this Lay Servant Ministries Advanced Course on storytelling is to acquaint lay servants with the history, art, selection, preparation, and presentation of stories in a variety of settings. More specifically, it is also to prepare lay servants for ministry through storytelling.

Each lay servant will

- tell a brief story from personal experience;
- develop and retell a brief story based on a parable of Jesus;
- relate, in a small-group setting, a personal account of a spiritual event;
- select a story to be developed and then told during the final session;
- offer support to other participants.

Keep in mind that this is an Advanced Course in the Lay Servant Ministries program, not an advanced course in storytelling. Some lay servants will have an interest in storytelling with little or no experience. Others will have had considerable experience in a variety of settings. While this course will offer some thing for all levels of storytellers, it is intended to equip lay servants with the fundamental skills and concepts used by storytellers. As a course leader, you will be responsible for keeping the sessions focused on the goals of the course and for being an encourager.

Our basic text is *Dancing With Words: Storytelling as Legacy, Culture, and Faith*, by Ray Buckley (Discipleship Resources, 2003). It is important that each participant have a copy of the book well in advance of the first meeting. As you contact class members with course information, ask them to read the entire text before arriving. It will assist you in being able to spend more time on storytelling rather than on reviewing the bulk of information in the text.

Much of the actual course will focus on formative exercises rather than explaining the text. It is important that participants be familiar with all of the text in order to maximize the helpfulness of the exercises. *Dancing With Words* will be a valuable aid as each lay servant continues her or his studies and practices of storytelling.

Dancing With Words will provide a wide range of ideas to assist lay servants with developing tools for storytelling. Many colleges, universities, seminaries, and summer programs offer classes and programs in storytelling. This text, designed for those working in faith communities, focuses additionally on the character of the storyteller, finding a sense of self, and awakening a sense of responsibility toward the listener. There is a strong emphasis on the spiritual element of storytelling. Part of your role as course leader is to create a positive environment that also enables individuals to experience storytelling in a worshipful, self-affirming manner. To help you accomplish this, consider doing the following things.

Affirm the positive. There will always be areas for improvement. In the short time you have allotted, focus on the good elements of the story and the storyteller.

Ask questions. Answering questions enables each participant to arrive at his or her own decisions regarding the process. Try, "If you had more time, what elements might you have added to the story?" or "How might you change the ending to slightly alter the story?"

or "What props might you use to make the story more visual?" Asking a directive question prevents you or other participants from making declarative statements ("It might have been more interesting had you used props") and encourages the exploration of the storyteller.

Provide a nurturing atmosphere. A nurturing atmosphere is one that includes planned activities in such a manner that people of all talent and experience levels benefit equally. Having a nurturing atmosphere means that as a group you are supportive of one another, so that each member benefits from the dynamic of the group. Watch for special needs. Pair the experienced with the inexperienced.

Remember that names are important. Nametags will probably be provided, but if you are like most of us, you have to put on your glasses to see them. For the time that you share a space, have large cards to place in front of you, simply folded in half with the first name of participants. It will help everyone.

Maintain the integrity of the program. Some structure is needed in every teaching environment. Follow the session plan as much as possible so that the preparation time of both you and the participants will be maximized. This is particularly important to the process of storytelling.

Create a sacred space. Notice that I said sacred, not scared! Hopefully your group is not large. Smaller groups work best in learning and refining storytelling. If the room is long and narrow, arrange the work space lengthwise, with ample room for yourself and for storytelling sessions. Define the space for your group. Some members may be telling elements of their personal stories for the first time. Covenant to preserve the sacredness of not only what is shared but also each person. In this place, everyone is treated with dignity and support.

Sacred space should also be appealing to the senses. The less sterile the atmosphere, the more creative your students will be. Consider having music playing before each session. Storybooks, a lighted candle, storytelling props, even a plant will create a warm environment and remove the feeling of a classroom.

Observe. Which cultural backgrounds are represented within your group? What other factors may influence group dynamics? If anyone expresses a cultural reluctance to a specific activity, or a genuine personal fear, find a way to include him or her. These are good exercises for storytelling in different settings.

DETAILS MATTER

Are you an experienced storyteller? If so, wonderful! You will have good instincts about the room, training, and making others feel welcome in storytelling.

Some Lay Servant Ministries training events are limited to a weekend, where five two-hour sessions are taught in succession. Some annual conferences allow different courses to be taught on their own schedule. Here are some thoughts to consider for this course on storytelling:

- If you have the option, *storytelling is best taught over an extended period of time.* Participants are then able to develop various styles and techniques as well as to find and develop various stories.

To the Course Leader

continued

- *Practice time is important.* Storytelling is a little like ballet. Well, that's stretching a bit! It does, however, require familiarity with the basics and development of skills, leading to good performance.
- *Feedback is important.* Developing storytellers (as well as advanced storytellers) appreciate time with peers. Successes and failures are good things to share.

If your time is limited to one weekend, you will not have as much time to practice, develop new techniques and applications, and exchange experiences. No matter what your time limits, though, think about offering something more! Consider establishing a storytelling fellowship or gathering where participants can meet occasionally and share ideas, joys, and frustrations as well as learn new skills. Lay Servant Ministries training in storytelling need not (should not) be a one-time opportunity. Those who are interested in expanding their skills will be delighted with the opportunity to continue both the exchange and the fellowship with one another.

As much as possible, keep classes small. Although larger classes will be appropriate for discussing the history, culture, philosophy, and techniques of story telling, it will become more difficult for actual storytelling if the group is too large. If you find your self with a group larger than desirable, consider these options:

- Identify qualified storytellers who may be recruited as assistants. It is always wonderful to have assistance. Having storytellers on hand will mean that more personal assistance can be given to each student.
- Divide the class into smaller groups for some activities. You will be able to accomplish more in smaller, intimate groups.

COMMITMENTS

Your sessions will be more productive if you ask each participant to make several commitments. Consider these as necessary obligations:

- attend every session (course credit cannot be given without it);
- arrive on time;
- stay until the session is complete;
- complete all assignments;
- maintain confidence;
- be encouraging.

The Lay Servant Ministries program, through Discipleship Ministries of The United Methodist Church, is a program of accreditation. It is essential that local congregations, districts, and annual conferences can depend on the integrity of the program. Participants need to be aware that accreditation depends upon their commitment to the program.

In addition to reading the text in advance, ask each participant to come to the event prepared to share:

- a three-minute story about an incident or a person from his or her own life;
- a three-minute retelling of a favorite parable of Jesus (other than the Prodigal Son);
- a seven-minute story of her or his own choosing to practice and tell during the final session.

To the Course Participant

DEAR LAY SERVANT IN TRAINING,

Welcome!

As an experienced lay servant, you are familiar with the variety of ministries available through the Lay Servant Ministries program. This Advanced Course will offer you both an overview of the importance of storytelling and opportunities for sharing your personal stories, as well as other stories. You will have an opportunity to

- tell a brief story from personal experience;
- develop and retell a brief story based on a parable of Jesus;
- relate, in a small-group setting, a personal account of a spiritual event;
- select a story before arriving to be developed and then told during the final session;
- offer support to other participants.

You are important to this learning experience! The stories you bring with you will enrich the lives of every one with whom you share. The stories of others will make you a richer person. We are glad that we will have this experience together.

Our basic text is *Dancing With Words: Storytelling as Legacy, Culture, and Faith*, by Ray Buckley (Discipleship Resources, 2003). Before you arrive for our time together, read the text fully. You will need to be familiar with much of it in preparation for this course. In addition, we are covenanting with each other to

- attend every session (course credit cannot be given without it);
- arrive on time;
- stay until each session is complete;
- complete all assignments;
- maintain confidence;
- be encouraging.

We will be meeting together for five two-hour sessions (or an equivalent time planned by your conference). Here are the dates, times, and location:

Dates	Time	Location

As we offer stories to one another, you will be asked to participate in a process designed to accomplish the most in the time we have together. A key portion of our time together will be supporting one another during this process, valuing the unique lives and experiences we bring to the group.

Storytelling is a fun experience. It can also be a personal, intimate, life-changing experience. Come with a prayer that God will bless our talents, give new insight, and provide a vision for ministry. Come most of all with an expectation that God will accomplish great things with our lives.

Together in ministry,

Session 1: The Legacy of Storytelling

TO THE PARTICIPANT

The purposes of this session are

- to examine the history and value of storytelling;
- to look at storytelling in the Bible.

Preparation for Session 1: You will have read *Dancing With Words* by now. Review the Introduction and Part I: The Legacy of Storytelling through the section related to storytelling and healing ending on page 26.

Come to the first session (and every session) with a Bible, having selected a favorite parable of Jesus. Bring with you your copy of *Dancing With Words*, a notepad for taking notes, and a copy of the parable you have selected.

TO THE LEADER

Before This Session: Make certain that each participant has a copy of *Dancing With Words: Storytelling as Legacy, Culture, and Faith.*

Check the room where you will be meeting to make sure that all of your supplies are in place. You will need a flip chart or dry-erase board; removable tape; markers in several colors; cardstock for name cards; extra notepads and pens; your Bible; your copy of *Dancing With Words*; a list of the participants; and information about restrooms, break times, public phones, and the location of refreshments. A three minute egg timer can also be useful.

Write the questions for group discussion in Step #3, "Examine the Heritage of Storytelling," on the flip chart or dry-erase board.

SESSION PLAN

1. **Opening the Session** (5 minutes)

Welcome the participants to the session. Briefly introduce yourself. Make certain that everyone has a text and the needed material. Go over the schedule, making sure that everyone has a copy.

2. **Worship** (25 minutes)

Consider using Psalm 78:1-4, from the Introduction to *Dancing With Words* (page 12). Take a moment for prayer.

Now it is time to really introduce yourself. Tell about an incident from your life that has significance for you. Shortly, the participants will be telling their own stories.

During the course of this session, intersperse various discussions with personal stories from one or two participants. If your group is small, ask each person to share something significant from her or his own experience that has personal meaning. The story or illustration should be from personal experience, and it should be true. With a three-minute egg timer you can help one another stay within a limited time.

Depending on the size of your group, ask several participants to tell their stories now, letting others tell theirs during the following sessions. It will be helpful to have them stand, or you may offer the use of a stool.

3. **Examine the Heritage of Storytelling** (25 minutes)
From the Introduction to the text, review briefly what happens to the human body when a story is told.

Ask participants to relate their memories of listening to stories as children. What was meaningful about those times? Who were the key storytellers?

Talk about the significance of face-to-face communication as discussed in the Introduction.

Using a flip chart or a dry-erase board, ask the group to respond to some basic questions: How often are we engaged in face-to-face communication? Where are the places we find community? How do we strengthen our personal relationships and our communities?

If you have people of varying backgrounds and ethnicity in your group, ask if they would be willing to share some information regarding storytellers and storytelling in their communities. **Note:** People from diverse ethnic or cultural backgrounds may not have access to or information about their traditional culture. Their experiences may be exactly like others in the class. Cultural backgrounds may also include geographical regions and religions.

Take a moment to talk about the role of traditional storytellers and the transmission of culture through story. If your class has enough members, have them divide themselves into subgroups of two or three. For a period of about ten minutes ask each subgroup to discuss the storytelling traditions of Native people, African-Americans, Australian Aboriginal people, those of Jewish communities, Hispanics, Europeans, Asians, and other peoples. (See *Dancing With Words*, pages 15-18.) Ask each subgroup to discuss such questions as:

- What is important about storytelling in each group? Are there other groups of which you are **aware**?
- How did these groups continue their traditions of storytelling?
- What contributions did various ethnic/regional groups make in the reemergence of storytelling?

Bring the class back together and ask each subgroup to share its ideas with the class.

4. **Break** (10 Minutes)

5. **Stories and the Faith Community** (15 minutes)
As the group comes back together, invite two people to tell their three-minute personal experience stories.

Briefly review oral tradition and Scripture. What is oral tradition? What role did oral tradition play in the development of the Old Testament? What was the role of storytellers in biblical cultures? (See *Dancing With Words*, pages 21-22.)

Discuss the importance of storytelling in the preaching ministry of Jesus. (See *Dancing With Words*, pages 22-24.)

Looking back at earlier discussions, ask the group to hypothesize about why crowds responded to the stories of Jesus.

6. **Storysharing** (20 minutes)
Divide the participants into subgroups of three. Using the egg timer, ask each person to retell one of the parables of Jesus other than the parable of the prodigal and his brother. Move around the room and spend time with each subgroup.

7. **Stories and Healing** (15 minutes)
As the group comes back together, ask participants to briefly relate how stories (whether formally told or simply related) have brought healing to their own personal lives or to the life of someone they know. What stories have brought hope or encouragement? Were they Bible stories or testimonials? Were they other stories? Were they stories told through literature or film?

Note to leaders and participants: It is important to limit the amount of time that each individual has for telling his or her stories. As many people as possible will need time for expression. Be sensitive to everyone. As awkward as it may seem, storytellers, even those who are sharing personally, have time limits. Encouraging participants to limit their time is important to the process of developing good story telling skills.

When this portion is complete, have the group offer prayers for joys and concerns.

8. **Assignments** (5 minutes)
For the next session, ask each participant to reread the end of Part I of the text, beginning with the section headed "Preaching and Storytelling."

Session 2: Storytelling as Preaching and Testimony

TO THE PARTICIPANT

The purposes of this session are

- to examine storytelling as preaching;
- to look at testimony as storytelling;
- to understand what makes a good story.

Preparation for Session 2: Review the end of Part I: The Legacy of Storytelling, beginning with the section "Preaching and Storytelling."

Reread Part II: The Story.

Recall a significant spiritual event or lesson from your own life that you are comfortable telling to a small group. Think about how you may relate it in five minutes.

TO THE LEADER

In this session you and the group will conclude Part I of *Dancing With Words* and begin Part II: The Story. Your main focus will be on the use of story as preaching and on the most basic form of story: eyewitness account or testimony.

In a very real sense, group members have already begun the process of testimony by telling the group something with significant meaning that is personally relevant. Both of these exercises will help develop a sense of comfort in speaking in front of a group.

Where you are to place information on a flip chart or dry-erase board, consider preparing these in advance as much as possible.

SESSION PLAN

1. **Worship and Introduction** (15 minutes)
Begin with a brief story of your own selection and a prayer. Ask another participant to tell his or her personal story.

2. **Storytelling and Preaching** (25 minutes)
Review the story of the young African seminarian from the text (*Dancing With Words*, page 27). What does it mean to be a responsible storyteller in a worship setting? On a flip chart or dry-erase board, list briefly some relevant points from the survey on preaching and storytelling (pages 27-28 in the text). Consider these:

- People who took notes could recall most of the sermon, but they had little memory of face-to-face impressions.
- Without stories, most parishioners could not recall the major points of a sermon one week later.
- Most congregants could recall stories or illustrations and how they related to the message, but they could not always remember the text.
- When storytelling became the main tool in the message, most individuals could recall all of the stories.

Session 2: Storytelling as Preaching and Testimony

continued

- Those who did not take notes could describe both the story and a series of emotional responses to the stories.
- Many pastors found the preparation time needed for the telling of stories to be more extensive than the preparation time needed for a traditional three point message.
- Almost all the pastors noticed that their congregations were more relaxed and attentive when stories were told.

Have a brief group discussion about the study. Why were the experiences of the note-takers and the non note-takers different? What conclusions can we draw from the comparison of these two groups? What storytelling dynamics took place between the pastor and the congregation?

Ask the participants to divide themselves into subgroups of three. It is important, as much as possible, to create different subgroups in each session. Earlier we shared three-minute brief stories. Have each subgroup member share a five-minute testimony of a significant spiritual event in her or his life. Why was this event significant?

3. **Break** (10 minutes)

4. **Characteristics of a Good Story** (45 minutes)

Ask the group this question: If you were going on a long journey and were able to take only one personal memento, other than family photos and your Bible, what would you take and why? For ten minutes, have the group stand and have participants ask the question to as many other people as possible, while **sharing their own "stories."**

Call the group back together and have them identify the various places where stories are found. Ask for a volunteer to write them down on a flip chart or dry-erase board. Keep the speed up, encouraging a flow of ideas. Ask for a few volunteers to share stories that have been handed down through their families. Allow about twenty minutes for this brain storming and storytelling.

Now, briefly review the elements of a good story (*Dancing With Words*, pages 39-40). Write the elements down in large letters on separate sheets of paper and place them around the room. While you do so, ask individuals from the group to describe each element:

- a clearly identifiable theme;
- a strong plot;
- strong character development;
- consistent style;
- elements of drama or surprise;
- appropriateness to age, audience, and so forth.

5. **Adapting Stories** (20 minutes)

Spend a few moments reviewing the importance of being accurate with the sources of our stories. Using stories from other cultures requires research into the culture. Finding a strong story does not always mean it is appropriate to use it. Do your homework. Consider:

- Where is this story from?

- Do I have the right to tell it?
- Am I being as true to the tradition as possible?
- Can I tell someone else's personal story?
- What is public domain?
- Who owns a story?

What are the considerations for using stories from the Bible?

- What does it mean to be true to the text?
- Is telling an "it might have happened" story based on a biblical theme okay?

Choose a story from the Bible—any story. Ask the class to consider various ways to present it, being:

- true to the text;
- age-appropriate;
- aware of cultural and historical information that may need to be explained.

An alternative to the above exercise would be to divide the group into subgroups and have each one work separately on a different set of questions.

6. **Assignments** (5 minutes)

Reread Part III: The Storyteller in *Dancing With Words*.

Review the story you will present in the final session, focusing on the areas of plot, characters, style, contrast/drama, and appropriateness.

Session 3: The Storyteller

TO THE PARTICIPANT

The purposes of this session are

- to begin preparation of your story;
- to understand and appreciate your importance in storytelling;
- to claim the process of learning a story.

Preparation for Session 3: Reread Part Ill: The Storyteller in the main text.

At the end of this course, you will be telling a story. You will have about seven minutes. In some ways it will be similar to the casual stories you have shared with your group. Over the next few sessions you will be looking at your own story as we examine story telling. Bring a written copy of your story to this session and to each session following.

TO THE LEADER

In *Dancing With Words*, Part III: The Storyteller, is the story "The Pool" (pages 49-50). Before the session, ask two participants to divide the story and read it aloud for the group.

Beginning in this session, participants will begin doing some of the individual preparation for telling their stories. Now is also an important time to affirm the gifts that God has given all of us for God's work. A good portion of that affirmation lies in believing that God has unique work that only you can do. This session involves both affirmation and application.

If you are a storyteller, consider sharing a story with the group. If you know of another storyteller who is willing to attend this session, this would be an excellent session to have a guest. One of the best ways to learn storytelling is to observe storytelling.

For this session, you will need to bring enough blank white paper to give each participant at least ten sheets.

SESSION PLAN

1. **Worship** (10 minutes)

Ask the two participants who have prepared for reading "The Pool" aloud to begin the session with that story.

End with a brief prayer of thanks for the uniqueness of each person in the room.

2. **Individual Story Preparation-I** (30 minutes)

Ask participants to work individually. Each will have brought the story he or she would like to tell in the final session. Ask them to break down the story by looking at the first four elements of a good story. Have them write their observations about the following questions pertaining to their stories.

- In ten sentences or fewer, can you describe the plot of the story?
- How many characters are there? Who are the main characters? In one sentence describe each one.

- What is the style of this story (biblical, folk, interactive, and so forth)?
- What is the source of this story?
- Where are the elements of drama, contrast, or surprise?
- What might you need to do to make this story appropriate for this audience?

3. **A Story** (10 minutes)
Have the storyteller you have invited tell his or her story. Or, tell a story yourself.

4. **Individual Story Preparation-II** (10 minutes)
Here is an assignment. Have each member of the class get up and walk, somewhere, anywhere, reading his or her story out loud (softly) while moving. Explain that while they are walking alone, they should simply pace themselves and read for ten minutes only.

Two rules: Do not run into each other. Do not walk in or near streets!

5. **Break** (10 minutes)

6. **Preparing Yourself for the Story** (20 minutes)
Using a flip chart, write the keys to helping yourself prepare for the story, each one on a separate page:

- Absorb the story.
- Identify areas of personal interest.
- Visualize the story.
- Add the senses.
- Look for key phrases.

From what they have read in *Dancing With Words* and from personal experience, have the group call out ways to assist the storyteller in each area. Write them on the appropriate pages. As each page is complete, place it somewhere on the wall of the room. Encourage quick responses to keep the pace moving.

7. **Setting the Scenes** (25 minutes)
Pass out the blank sheets of paper so that everyone has an ample supply (at least ten sheets per person).

In the remaining few minutes of this session, have each participant create images of his or her story. In the tradition of a slide show or flannel board, each story should be broken down into scenes.

This exercise is not an art contest. Stick figures are just fine, as long as you know what you mean!

This will be an unfamiliar exercise for many. Encourage participants to give this exercise their best effort. They will be using these images to practice for the later sessions.

8. **Assignments** (5 minutes)
Reread Part IV: Listeners and Hearers-Storysharing.

Practice telling your story using the pictures you drew during Session 3.

Session 4: Storysharing

TO THE PARTICIPANT

The purposes of this session are

- to prepare for the storytelling event;
- to understand proper speaking and storytelling technique;
- to effectively engage an audience.

Preparation for Session 4: Reread Part IV: Listeners and Hearers—Storysharing. Practice telling your story several times.

You have been preparing your story for presentation. In this session we will look at several ideas to help you be a better public speaker in general and a storyteller in particular. These are not techniques to be mastered quickly, but this course is a good place to begin. You will be asked to apply these principles to the story you are going to share and to think about ways to integrate them into your storytelling experience.

TO THE LEADER

Find a couple of standalone mirrors to use today. There are a number of physical exercises in this session, and it helps to be able to see how you are doing! Many of these experiences will seem new, and perhaps overwhelming. What we are focusing on is not everything at once, but little steps—a good beginning.

Has everyone had an opportunity to share her or his personal story or parable retelling? If not, intersperse some more during the course of the session. The goal is to have each participant telling an informal story in front of a small group as often as possible.

As the course moves more into public performance, it is important that each student see his or her role as that of an encourager. We are here to uplift each other. Any other kind of behavior is not acceptable in a nurturing environment. Remember the commitments?

SESSION PLAN

1. **Worship and More** (15 minutes)

Sing! "Great Is Thy Faithfulness" is an excellent choice for this session. Invite those who are able to stand.

When you have sung the song through, ask the group to remain standing. Consider saying, in your own words, "Stand with your feet shoulder-width apart. Begin with your arms at your side, then lift them straight above your head until they are pointing toward the sky. Slowly lower your arms, breathing deeply as you do. Imagine that there is a string coming from the back of your head, lifting straight upward. Pretend that there is also a string coming from the middle of your chest, lifting straight upward. Your chin should be parallel with your feet. Breathe in slowly through your nose to a slow count of eight. Hold your breath for four counts. Exhale slowly for eight counts. Then breathe normally."

Sing the first verse of "Great Is Thy Faithfulness" again—this time without books. You may help the class with the words.

Stand for another moment; then say a brief prayer.

2. **Public Speaking and Storytelling** (20 minutes)

Most of the participants will be familiar with the key elements of good public speaking. These are, how ever, at the same time the things easiest to overlook and the most important. Spend a little time reminding the class of the significance of each of these elements:

- projection—the need to be heard without straining your voice;
- facial expressions—making sure you are projecting what you wish;
- voice modulation and speed—creating interest with your voice;
- silence—creating drama or intensity;
- repetition—helping the audience remember;
- defining characters—making changes in presentation as you change characters.

3. **Practicing** (25 minutes)

Allow the group to practice their stories individually. Suggest using the mirrors or finding rooms where mirrors might be available. Where might each participant think her or his story could be infused with appropriate facial expression, voice modulation, silence, and so forth? Practice!

4. **Break** (10 minutes)

5. **Partners** (25 minutes)

Divide the class into groups of two. Ask each person to tell his or her story to his or her partner. One partner will serve as a timekeeper and observer. The role of the partner is to offer not critique but encouragement.

When the story is complete, the partner/listener will ask questions of the storyteller. Here are some good questions a partner might ask:

- What were you happy with?
- Were there some things you would like to have done differently?

Some affirming statements a partner might make are:

- I especially liked ...
- These are the things that impressed me the most ...
- When you did ____________, I felt ____________

6. **The Audience** (18 minutes)

Review briefly the section headed "Attitude Is Every thing" (*Dancing With Words*, pages 84-85).

Remove all other notes and flip chart pages from the walls. On one piece of paper, list these phrases:

- Choose a story that you believe in.
- Reduce the story to the elements most important to you.
- Wrap yourself in the story.
- Be yourself.
- Prepare yourself for the story.

Session 4: Storysharing

continued

- Be confident.

Take a moment to review each of these phrases with the participants.

Leave this list in the room for the final session.

7. Assignments (2 minutes)

Remind the class that the last session will be reserved for them to tell their stories.

Have the group gather in a circle and conclude with a word of prayer.

Session 5: Telling Our Stories

TO THE PARTICIPANT

The purpose of this session is

- To be able to tell the story you have selected in a safe, encouraging, warm, and sacred atmosphere. It is not to be a great performer. It is not to be perfect. It is to share both yourself and the story that gives you joy. It is also to share it with people who have become your friends.

Preparation for Session 5: Practice, practice, practice! Pray and offer encouragement to others.

TO THE LEADER

You will determine how this last session is developed. Consider making the room informal. Now is the time to light a candle. Fire in most cultures signifies welcome and warmth. Have a chair or a stool available. If you have the option, create a storytelling set: a comfortable chair or stool next to a small table, with a candle and some books. Toss in a plant. It will make a difference and make everyone feel special.

Although the participants will finally be sharing their stories, you are the key to the success of this session. Each of the points you have listed on flip-charts or dry-erase boards during all of the sessions will help you direct the participants in evaluating their own stories.

SESSION PLAN

1. Worship (5 minutes)

Open with a brief worship. Sing a song. Gather the group in a circle and read a passage of Scripture. Sing another song. Have a brief word of prayer.

2. Review (10 minutes)

Remember the notes you left on the flip chart page last session? Have the class read them aloud together. Repetition!

3. Storytelling (90 minutes)

If your group is fairly large, you will probably need the entire time for storytelling, with a break in the middle. If the group is smaller in size, you have more options. Consider having participants tell their stories twice, with a break in between. They will be more at ease the second time, and you will have time for individual encouragement.

Remember to use the directive questions and the positive statements you used with partners. It is always more effective to point out things done well and then with directive questions allow the storyteller to draw his or her own conclusions. Nothing is better than thinking of it yourself!

After each story allow group members to express their own **positive** remarks. Emphasize that only positive comments are needed.

After you have led the way with directive questioning and the group has shared positive remarks, make some comments regarding the story itself. Here you have some different opportunities. Critiquing a story teller is different from critiquing a story. Use phrases like:

"I was captivated by _______ and wanted more! What might you do to add some additional elements to this portion of the story?"

4. **Closing** (15 minutes)
At the end of the session (it's been a busy time) allow for a free time of questions, comments, observations, and ideas.

As you wrap up this formal time of training, affirm each person in the class.

Conclude with a prayer in which everyone's name is mentioned.

A Prayer for Storytellers

0 God,
My God.
Words are small,
but you are The Word.
You are words upon words, upon words,
spinning like stars in the heaven,
creating new visions, new dreams,
new ways of seeing my world.
You are the actualization of all words.
You are the beginning and end of The Story,
all stories,
my story.
Be the originator of my words;
your faithfulness, my repetition.
Wrap me in your presence, your story,
until I wear you,
undisguised,
in all my words.
Amen

-rb

Additional Helpful Resources

Additional copies of this booklet (order number DR408), the text *Dancing With Words* (DR407), and other Lay Servant Ministries courses and texts can be ordered online at upperroombooks.com or by phone at 800-972-0433.

Books

The Art of the Story-Teller, by Marie L. Shedlock (Dover Publications, 1951). A storytelling classic. Rich ideas and insights from one of the premier storytellers of the twentieth century.

Just Enough to Make a Story, by Nancy Schimmel (Sisters' Choice Press, 1992). Strong suggestions for delivery.

Look What Happened to Frog: Storytelling in Education, by Pamela J. Cooper and Rives Collins (Gorsuch Scarisbrick, 1992). Highlights include suggestions for effective delivery and developing your own style.

Once Upon a Time: A Storytelling Handbook, by Lucille N. Breneman and Bren Breneman (Nelson-Hall Publishers, 1983). Highlights include suggestions for developing characterization, the use of visualization in storytelling, audience eye contact, and body language.

The Storytellers Start-Up Book, by Margaret Read Mac Donald (August House, 1993).

Storytelling Step by Step, by Marsh Cassady (Resource Publications, 1990). Provides good insight into using personal experiences in storytelling and has an excellent chapter on delivery. This publisher has produced several works for storytelling in faith-based situations.

The Way of the Storyteller, by Ruth Sawyer (Viking Press, 1942). Good tools for delivery and moving past "technique."

Website

Lay Servant Ministries: www.layservant.org

Printed in the USA
CPSIA information can be obtained
at www.ICGtesting.com
JSHW060022070424
60532JS00003B/14

9 780881 774085